The Rock Paper Scissors Handbook

by the World Rock Paper Scissors Association

www.wrpsa.com

© 2017 WRPSA

Written By: Wyatt Baldwin

TABLE OF CONTENTS

INTRODUCTION

You might think do we really need a Rock Paper Scissors Handbook. Yes, Rock Paper Scissors is the greatest hand game in the world. It is the most commonly played and easiest to learn. It can be used to settle a debate or just for fun. There is no language needed and no set-up required. A game that some may think is similar to a coin flip, in this book you will learn it is far more than that.

This book is intended to provide you with all the information you will ever need about the great sport of Rock Paper Scissors. In doing this our goal is that you are able to realize your full potential. Learn the Rules, Strategies, Gambit Play, what Game Theory is and how it can be applied to Rock Paper Scissors. Along with Psychology, Etiquette and all the Jokes we could think of and find for this incredible sport.

The World Rock Paper Scissors Association (WRPSA) was created to bring honesty and integrity back to the most played hand game in the world and intended to provide stability for the hand sport where no organization has in the past. We are the preferred destination for anyone interested in the sport of Rock Paper Scissors. We have spent years playing and researching this sport, everything we have learned about Rock Paper Scissors is included in this Handbook.

WHAT IS ROCK PAPER SCISSORS AND IS IT FAIR?

Rock Paper Scissors is one of the oldest hand games still played today. Hand Games have a long history incivilization dating back to the Chinese Han Dynasty (206 BC – 220 AD). People play Rock Paper Scissors to settle arguments; anyone who wins is accepted to be the winner of the argument or help decide what choices to make between two available options.

There are no restrictions to that restrict who can play Rock Paper Scissors (RPS). There is no age limit, no gender limitation, and no racial discrimination as to who can play. Rock Paper Scissors is for everybody as far as you are mentally sound and can reason then Rock Paper Scissors is for you.

In fact, Rock Paper Scissors is a game that builds one's mental reasoning; it helps you think fast and make the right decisions even in real life circumstances. Playing Rock Paper Scissors is a way of unwinding and exercising the brain at the same time.

Have you ever wondered who can play Rock Paper Scissors? The answer would be Students, Adults, Professionals, Men, Women, Boys and Girls. It will not be out of place to say EVERYBODY can play. It is all about studying the psychology of your opponent and predicting what they will do next and how they react to what you do so it is an interesting game

4

that can help the brain. It is all about thinking, strategizing, decision making among others.

When it comes to the area of being fair, it depends on your perspective or definition of fair, because absolute fairness could only be achieved by an entirely arbitrary mechanic, which make for a lousy game. However, in my opinion, RPS is likely the fairest game around for the following five reasons:

- It requires no equipment other than a single functioning hand and therefore has no bias towards the wealthy who can afford better equipment or training.
- Performance in the game is not improved by drugs, which evens the playing field between players who choose to use a performance-enhancing drug and those who choose to play "clean".
- The game does not favor any specific body type, age or gender. Strength and speed are not of any real significance.
- The game is so simple to grasp that all but the most significantly mentally-challenged players can understand the rules completely.
- The game has no ambiguity (Rock always beats scissors, etc.) nor is the game judged by any third-party (like many Olympic sports), which means that any honest player or observer will always concur on the outcome.

Therefore, the only real differentiator between the players is how well they choose, so it favors those who can read their opponents, mask their intentions and think strategically, but isn't that the essence of a game? Of course it is, and i am yet to see a game that is not all about trying to out-smart your opponent. If there is any then I will agree that Rock Paper Scissors is not fair.

THE HISTORY OF ROCK PAPER SCISSORS

Rock Paper Scissors has been around for a long time, and most civilized people have at least a passing knowledge of the game, here is the history of our sport.

The first known mention of the game was in the book Wuzazu written by the Chinese Ming-dynasty writer Xie Zhaozhi who wrote that the game dated back to the time of the Chinese Han dynasty (206 BC – 220 AD). In the book, the game was called shoushiling. Li Rihua's book Note of Liuyanzhai also mentions this game, calling it shoushiling, huozhitou, or huoquan.

Throughout Japanese history there are frequent references to "sansukumi-ken", meaning "ken" fist games with a "san" three-way "sukumi" deadlock. This is in the sense that A beats B, B beats C, and C beats A. The games originated in China before being imported to Japan and subsequently becoming popular.

The earliest Japanese "sansukumi-ken" game was known as "mushi-ken", which was imported directly from China. In "Mushi-ken" the "frog" (represented by the thumb) is superseded by the "slug" (represented by the little finger), which, in turn is superseded by the "snake" (represented by the index finger), which is superseded by the "frog". Although this game was imported from China the Japanese version differs in the animals represented. In adopting the game, the original Chinese characters for the poisonous centipede were apparently confused with the characters for the "slug". The most popular sansukumi-ken game in Japan was kitsune-ken. In the game, a supernatural fox called a kitsune defeats the village head, the village head defeats the hunter, and the hunter defeats the fox. Kitsune-ken, unlike mushi-ken or rock–paper–scissors, is played by making gestures with both hands.

Frog   Snake   Slug

The Creation of Rock Paper Scissors

The earliest form of Rock Paper Scissors was created in Japan and is called janken, which is a variation of the Chinese games introduced in the 17th century. Janken uses the rock, paper, and scissors signs and is the game that the modern version of rock paper scissors derives from directly. Hand-games using gestures to represent the three conflicting elements of rock, paper, and scissors have been most common since the modern version of the game was created in the late 19th century, between the Edo and Meiji periods.

By the early 20th century, rock paper scissors had spread beyond Asia, especially through increased Japanese contact with the west. Its English-language name is therefore taken from a translation of the names of the three Japanese hand-gestures for rock, paper and scissors: elsewhere in Asia the open-palm gesture represents "cloth" rather than "paper". The shape of the scissors is also adopted from the Japanese style.

Spread beyond Asia

In Britain in 1924 it was described in a letter to The Times as a hand game, possibly of Mediterranean origin, called "zhot". A reader then wrote in to say that the game "zhot" referred to was evidently Jan-ken-pon, which she had often seen  played throughout Japan. Although at this date the game appears to have been new enough to British readers to need explaining, the appearance by 1927 of a popular thriller with the title Scissors Cut Paper, followed by Stone Blunts Scissors (1929), suggests it quickly became popular.

In 1927 La Vie au patronage, a children's magazine in France, described it in detail, referring to it as a "jeu japonais" ("Japanese game"). Its French name, "Chi-fou-mi", is based on the Old Japanese words for "one, two, three" ("hi, fu, mi").

A New York Times article of 1932 on the Tokyo rush hour describes the rules of the game for the benefit of American readers, suggesting it was not at that time widely known in the U.S. The 1933 edition of the Compton's Pictured Encyclopedia described it as a common method of settling disputes between children in its article on Japan; the name was given as "John Kem Po" and the article pointedly asserted, "This is such a good way of deciding an argument that American boys and girls might like to practice it too."

Rock paper scissors is one of the few sansukumi ken games still played in modern Japan. It's uncertain why rock-paper-scissors managed to surpass the popularity of all other sansukumi-ken games. Everyone believes that the global success of rock-paper-scissors comes from the universal appeal of its simplicity. Unlike other sansukumi-ken games, rock-paper-scissors could be easily understood by any audience.

A Timeline of the History of Rock Paper Scissors

2016 BC - 220 AD

Chinese Ming - Dynasty writer Xie Zhaozhi (1567-1624) writes that a hand game called Shoudhling translated meaning "hand command" was played during the Han Dynasty.

17th Century

Mushi-Ken (Frog, Slug, Snake) was brought to Japan in the 17th century as a Chinese drinking game under the rame sansukumi-ken, which translates into "ken of the three who are afraid of another".

Late 19th Century

"Janken" is created. A hand game using gestured to represent the three conflicting elements of rock, paper and scissors are created between the Edo and Meiji periods.

Early 20th Century

Rock, Paper, Scissors had spread beyond Asia, especially through increased Japanese contact with the West.

1924

In Britain it was described in a letter to The Times as a hand game called "Zhot".

1927

La Vie au Patronage, a childrens magazine in France described the game as a Japanese game with the name "Chi-fou-mi", based on the Old Japanese words for one, two, three "hi, fu, mi".

1932

A New York Times has an that article describes the rules of rock paper scissors for the benefit of American readers.

1933

Compton's Pictured Encyclopedia described rock paper scissors as a common method of settling disputes between children.

HOW TO PLAY ROCK PAPER SCISSORS

Rock Paper Scissors is a hand game usually played between two people, in which each player simultaneously forms one of three shapes with an outstretched hand. These shapes are "rock" (a simple fist), "paper" (a flat hand), and "scissors" (a fist with the index and middle fingers together forming a V).

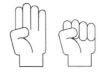

Rock Smashes Scissors   Scissors Cuts Paper   Paper Covers Rock

The players show their shapes on the 4th prime. This is after a count of 3 and on the verbal cue of 'Shoot' this can also be a non-verbal cue. If both players choose the same shape, the game is tied and is immediately replayed to break the tie. Players agree to the best of series prior to competing. In official WRPSA matches games are played in best 3 of 5.

The game is often used as a choosing method in a way similar to coin flipping, drawing straws, or throwing dice. Unlike truly random selection methods, however, Rock Paper Scissors can be played with a degree of skill by recognizing and exploiting non-random behavior in opponents.

The Rock: The rock is internationally recognized by a closed fist where the thumb is not concealed. It is also one of the most popular opening moves and this is why it is considered to be one of the most popular hand signals. Most players will view using the rock as an opening move to be somehow aggressive but would still use it because it is easy. The rock will beat scissors every time but will be beaten by paper.

The Paper: Paper is delivered in the same way as the rock except that in this case all the fingers and the thumb are extended in a way that they all face the same direction. The vertical paper or the handshake is strictly forbidden in tournaments of Rock Paper Scissors because it might resemble the scissors which can lead to unnecessary confusion. Paper is one of the most challenging opening moves because there is no indication of what you intend to do next. As a result, many players will be concerned when you use it as an opening move to your game. Paper will beat rock but will be beaten by scissors in no time.

The Scissors: Scissors are thrown in the same way as rock where the hand is clenched into a fist but the index and the middle finger are extended to the front in order to make an angle that is of 30 to 45 degrees in a way that would resemble a pair of scissors. The use of horizontal scissors is strictly forbidden in tournaments because they can resemble the shape of paper. Opening with scissors is not a very smart move because your opponent will be able to guess what your signal is going to be easily and so will be able to come up with a stronger signal.

It is very important to conceal your move and to surprise your opponent if you want to make sure that you will win this game.

ROCK PAPER SCISSORS TO SOLVE CONFLICTS

Here's a strategy to help kids move past disagreements that don't require solving or processing. From its 2000-year-old roots in China, Rock-Paper-Scissors came to be played all over the world in the 20th century. This hand game uses gestures to help kids decide who goes first, gets to choose, or "wins."

At the count of three, the players reach out with their hand in a fist (Rock), flat (Paper), or pointing two fingers (Scissors). Scissors cut paper; paper covers rock; rock 'smashes' scissors. Roshambo beautifully de-personalizes and takes the edge off all kinds of conflict. It's a random draw, a great and fun game that calls for no shouting or screaming.

Whenever there is a "Yes I am", "No you're not" conflict, the game Rock, Paper, Scissors Game Helps to settle the conflict. If you didn't learn Rock Paper Scissors as a child, learn it now and teach it to others. The more tools we have to prevent and deal with squabbles, the more harmonious and peaceful our lives can be.

Determine an order for doing something.

Rock, Paper, Scissors can also be handy for establishing what order things come in, like when you're fighting with your friends over who gets to be in the front of the line. You can even play several games between three or more people to set up a final order in advance. After each player has gone up against everyone else, tally up your total number of wins, using tie-breaker games as needed.

A few rounds of Rock, Paper, Scissors can help you set up an order faster than talking it out can.

Play for fun.

Even if there's nothing riding on the game, you can still play Rock, Paper, Scissors for your own enjoyment. Keep tally of you and your opponent's wins and losses, and play until one of you reaches a predetermined number. It's similar to Tic-Tac-Toe in that you can go through multiple games in a lightning-quick fashion. That spontaneity will help keep you on your toes!

Rock Paper Scissors isn't just a silly game kids play, this is serious stuff. It's psychological warfare and everyone can play this fun game for different reasons.

THE OFFICIAL RULES OF ROCK PAPER SCISSORS

Tournament Format

This will be a single-elimination tournament, best of five series to win. The first contestant to win three games shall be considered the winner of the match.

The Set up of the Game

Before the game starts, the players must agree upon what decision is to be made (and considered binding) as a result of the match. If no compromise or agreement could be struck and the players still wish to continue, then the match by default is considered to be an "honour" match.

The number of primes to be used is four. An audible couting ouf the primes 1, 2, 3, shoot may be used by the players. In recreational games alterations of this may be made and must be agreed between the two players.

The decision-makers must stand opposite each other with one outstretched fist at waist height with a distance between their fists of no less than 1 foot and no more than 4 feet.

In recreational games the players must agree on the number of rounds to be played before the match is concluded. If they can't reach an agreement on this, the game by defaults will be a single round format. Card carrying WRPSA members are able to determine the number of rounds in a match of RPS before a matchand it is considered to be binding (i.e., best of 3, best of 5, best of 161, etc.). The Card must be shown prior to play. For tournament play the number of rounds must be clearly stated by the referee.

Beginning the Play – Pre-Prime Phase

A "call for prime" is issued by one player to his/her opponent in a RAT (recognizable audible tone). A Recognizable Audible Tone, is defined as an utterance that can be heard by the challenging player. Using the word "ready" is considered good form.

In the case of match with or between hearing impared players or in situations where it is critical that silence must be maintained, a mutually agreement upon Recognizable Visual Signal can replace the standard RAT. In this case, a nod of the head while looking directly into the eyes of the other player is accepted as the standard form.

A 'return of the call" is then issued by the other player who thus acknowledges the "call for prime", also in a RVS (or RAT). Once the "return of the call" has been established, players are considered to be "at ready".

Play may begin anytime after the players are established and recognized as being "at ready".

The Game is considered to be "in play" after any player "breaks ready" and thus "initiates the prime"

Priming

The vertical prime is performed by retracting the outstretched fist back towards the players' shoulder (players must face each other and perform the prime with arms parallel).

The fist should be retracted towards the players' own body rather than your opponent's to avoid possible contact.

As soon as one player has "broken ready" and initiated the first prime, it is the responsibility and obligation of the opponent also to begin priming and to "synch" or "catch" the prime with the first player so they can establish a delivery and approach.

The player who has initiated the prime is under the strict obligation to maintain a constant priming speed so as to give his opponent every opportunity to "catch the prime"

The fist must remain in the closed position until the delivery of the final prime. The fist is the only acceptable hand position during the prime.

The fist must remain in full view of the opposing player and may not come in contact with any outside influences that inhibit the opponent's view.

Before the delivery of the final prime, the game may be called off for the following reasons only: decision clarification, rule clarification, or injury.

Approach

Once the fist has reached the highest point of the final throw of the last prime, the delivery of the throw is considered to be "in approach". At any time during the approach of this final prime, the hand may be released in any of the following manners:

 Rock: represented by a closed fist with the thumb resting at least at the same height as the topmost finger of the hand. The thumb must not be concealed by the fingers.

Note: To accommodate different throwing styles, it is considered legal for the first knuckle of the thumb to point downward.

Scissors: Is delivered in the same manner as rock with the exception that the index and middle fingers are fully extended toward the opposing player. It is considered good form to angle the topmost finger upwards and the lower finger downwards in order to create a roughly 30–45 degree angle between the two digits and thus mimic a pair of scissors.

Paper: Is also delivered in the same manner as rock with the exception that all fingers including the thumb are fully extended and horizontal with the points of the fingers facing the opposing player. Use of the "vertical paper" (sometimes referred to as "the handshake") is considered exceptionally bad form.

Throws must be delivered prior to the completion of the approach. The approach is considered finished when the forearm is at a 90-degree angle to the upper body. Any throw not delivered prior to the hand crossing the 90-degree mark shall be considered a throw of rock.

Delivery

Participants must exercise extreme caution, dexterity, and care not to initiate contact between the opposing fists during any point of the priming phase. The direct contact of the fists can cause chaffing, scraping, rapping of the knuckles. Make sure any onlookers are aware of the intentions of the players as the swinging of closed fists can be mistaken as a sign of a potentially combative situation.

Should direct contact occur players should stop play immediately and assess if there are any personal injuries before restarting the prime.

After players have revealed their throws play must stop until an agreement can be reached as to a winner or if a stalemate situation has arisen.

Throws

A game of Rock Paper Scissors can have only the following outcomes.

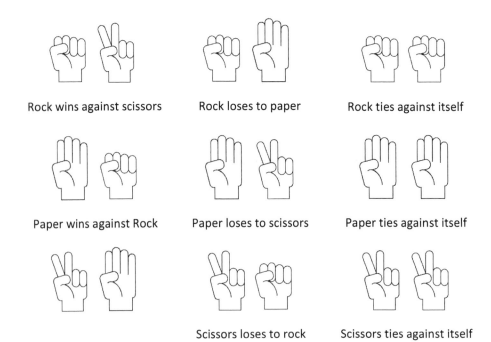

Rock wins against scissors	Rock loses to paper	Rock ties against itself
Paper wins against Rock	Paper loses to scissors	Paper ties against itself
	Scissors loses to rock	Scissors ties against itself

Scissors wins against

paper

Players may use any combination of these throws at any time throughout the match. Any throws that are not conforming to the standard hand positions (outlined above) and thus deemed to be a rock (stone), paper, or scissors is considered to be an illegal throw and it is forbidden. Should a player execute an illegal throw, the opposing player has the right (but not the obligation) to claim immediate victory over the round (not the match). Alternatively, the infringed upon player has the right but not the obligation to replay the current game if he/she so chooses.

The winner of the round is dictated by the player's throw which beats that of the opponent. Under no circumstances can a losing throw ever beat a winning throw.

In the case of a stalemate, where players reveal the same throw the round must be replayed. There are no limits to the numbers of stalemates which may occour in any given match. Should players find themselves in a continuous stalemate situation, also known as "Mirror Play", a good approach can be to take a short "timeout" to rethink your strategy.

Post Game Play

There is no limit to the number of rounds, matches, or games that can be played in RPS. The game may continue until any and all decisions are reached and is at the discretion of the players involved. Games for honour can be substituded at any point after the conclusion of a match as long as is agreed upon by all players involved before the beginning of the next match.

ROCK PAPER SCISSORS STRATEGIES

If you see someone who has always won the Rock Paper Scissors as being lucky, I think you need to have a rethink. It goes beyond being lucky as there are known techniques that can guarantee a consistent winning streak. I will be talking about some of this technique here.

In fact, consistently winning at Rock, Paper, Scissors only requires reading through a bit of strategy, and you'll be ready to win every challenge and throw. It is all about strategy

If your opponent loses to you on the first throw, then it becomes easy to predict their next move due to the human tendency towards conditional responses. It is normal for everybody.

The reason for this is because people are influenced by the choices they have previously made. If the previous choice did not work, it is always a natural tendency to try another choice.

One of the fundamentally known techniques to winning Rock Paper Scissors is to pay attention to your opponent's choices, and your chances of emerging a winner automatically increase.

There is no sure way to guarantee that you will win throw one, so just keep it simple: throw paper. Unless your opponent is also trained in the art of winning Rock Paper Scissors, you should have a better chance of winning because people choose to throw rock first more often than paper or scissors. If you've won the first round, great. You're on your way to victory.

What did your opponent throw on the first hand?

Whatever it was, choose the next item in the rotation of Rock - Paper - Scissors. People typically move through these three choices in order and are also very unlikely to repeat their losing choice. So, if your opponent chose paper, they will probably throw scissors next.

So, you should choose rock. If they chose scissors, they would probably choose rock, so you should choose paper.

If you lost the first round, don't panic. There's still hope. When someone wins, they're more likely to pick the same thing again because they feel that it was a good choice.

Remember this important rule about your opponent; if they won with scissors, you should pick rock to win the next throw, because chances are, they will pick scissors again. Remember this rule, and you will your chances of winning is higher.

Follow these three rules for playing the game, and your chances of winning Rock, Paper, Scissors will be high enough for you to take over the role as the "Lucky Friend" without anyone ever realizing how you did it.

The First Throw

Men tend to pick rock as their first throw, maybe because rocks are more of a stereotypically masculine symbol.

Women usually throw paper first. So if you're playing against a man, you should throw paper first; if you are playing with a woman, throw scissors.

After the First Loss

Once someone loses a round, they don't throw the same thing they just threw immediately after. In fact, they often throw the thing that beat them.

If someone lost by throwing a rock against paper, they would probably throw paper next. Knowing that can help you beat someone twice in a row.

A study from China's Zhejiang University found another pattern in what people throw after a loss. The study found a triangle of moves that people throw in order: "If your opponent lost with a rock, they would likely choose paper next. If they lost with paper, they'll choose scissors, and so on."

How to beat a winner

In general, people who win play the winning symbol again directly afterward, according to the Zhejiang University study. If your opponent just beat you with scissors, play rock against them next, because they will likely throw scissors again.

A Fun Trick

One way to throw people off is to announce what you're about to throw before you throw it; and then follow through. Your opponent won't trust you, and will be expecting you to throw anything other than what you announced.

Contrary to what you might think Rock Paper Scissors is not simply a game of luck or chance. While it is true that from a mathematical perspective the 'optimum' strategy is to play randomly, it still is not a winning strategy for two reasons.

First, 'optimum' in this case means you should win, lose and draw an equal number of times (hardly a winning strategy over the long term).

Second, Humans, try as they might, are terrible at trying to be random, in fact often humans in trying to approximate randomness become quite predictable. Knowing that there is always something motivating your opponent's actions, there are a couple of techniques and tricks that you can use to tip the balance in your favor.

Rock is for Rookies

In RPS circles a common mantra is "Rock is for Rookies" because males have a tendency to lead with Rock on their opening throw. It has a lot to do with idea that Rock is perceived as "strong" and forceful", so guys tend to fall back on it. Use this knowledge to take an easy first win by playing Paper.

The Bart Simpson

This strategy became famous with the broadcast of the "Front Door" episode of The Simpsons, where we heard Bart thinking to himself, "Good old rock. Can't beat rock." Then we heard Lisa thinking, "Poor predictable Bart. Always picks rock." Bart threw rock. Lisa threw paper. Lisa won. The "Bart Simpson" is probably the worst Janken strategy of all time.

Scissors on First

The second step in the 'Rock is for Rookies' line of thinking is to play scissors as your opening move against a more experienced player. Since you know they won't come out with rock (since it is too obvious), scissors is your obvious safe move to win against paper or stalemate to itself.

The Double Run

When playing with someone who is not experienced at the RPS, look out for double runs (the same throw twice). When this happens you can safely eliminate that throw and guarantee yourself at worst a stalemate in the next game. So, when you see a two-Scissor run, you know their next move will be Rock or Paper, so Paper is your best move. Why does this work? People hate being predictable and the perceived hallmark of predictability is to come out with the same throw three times in row.

Telegraph Your Throw

Tell your opponent what you are going to throw and then actually throw what you said. Why? As long as you are not playing someone who actually thinks you are bold enough to telegraph your throw and then actually deliver it, you can eliminate the throw that beats the throw you are telegraphing. So, if you announce rock, your opponent won't play paper which means coming out with that scissors will give you at worst a stalemate and at best the win.

Step Ahead Thinking

Don't know what to do for your next throw? Try playing the throw that would have lost to your opponents last throw? Sounds weird but it works more often than not, why? Inexperienced (or flustered) players will often subconsciously deliver the throw that beat their last one.

Therefore, if your opponent played paper, they will very often play Scissors, so you go Rock. This is a good tactic in a stalemate situation or when your opponent lost their last game. It is not as successful after a player has won the last game as they are generally in a more confident state of mind which causes them to be more active in choosing their next throw.

Suggest A Throw

When playing against someone who asks you to remind them about the rules, take the opportunity to subtly "suggest a throw" as you explain to them by physically showing them the throw you want them to play. ie "Paper beats Rock, Rock beats scissors (show scissors), Scissors (show scissors again) beats paper." Believe it or not, when people are not paying attention their subconscious mind will often accept your "suggestion". A very similar technique is used by magicians to get someone to take a specific card from the deck.

When All Else Fails Go With Paper

If you do not have a clue on what to throw next, then go with Paper. Why? Statistically, in competition play, it has been observed that scissors is thrown the least often. Specifically, it gets delivered 29.6% of the time, so it slightly under-indexes against the expected average of 33.33% by 3.73%. Obviously, knowing this only gives you a slight advantage, but in a situation where you just don't know what to do, even a slight edge is better than none at all.

The Rounder's Ploy

This technique seems more like 'cheating'. Hpwever, if you think all that matters is a win for you and you can live with it yourself the next day by defending your actions, then you can use it to get an edge. The way it works is when you suggest a game with your opponent, do not announce the number of rounds you are going to play. Play the first match and if you win, take it is as a win. If you lose, without missing a beat start playing the 'next' round on the assumption that it was a best 2 out of 3. No doubt you will hear protests from your opponent but stay firm and remind them that 'no one plays best of one for a kind of decision that you two are making'. No this devious technique won't guarantee you the win, but it will give you a chance to battle back to even and start again.

Physical Skills

The basic skills of RPS need no discussion. Most children can be taught to form the three throws with their hands and with a little practice can follow the prime and reveal their chosen throw at the appropriate time.

An advanced RPS player can do more than that. He can use his hands to confuse or deceive an opponent. She can make her opponent believe she is going to throw Rock when she is going to throw scissors.

Cloaking

"Cloaking" is the term used for delaying the unveiling of the throw. Put a little more simply, "Cloaking" is waiting until the last possible second to throw Paper or Scissors. Some players will watch your hands for an indication of which throw you are about to use. By not moving your fingers until the last moment, you can fool such a player into thinking you are throwing Rock. Since a hand-watcher will respond to a well-executed cloak with paper, cloaking Scissors is more useful than cloaking Paper.

Smoothing Tells

"Tells" are visible behaviors through which a player may unconsciously reveal a throw to an opponent. Everyone has them to some degree – they've been the poker player's friend and enemy for centuries. They are the reason that hand-watchers watch hands, but tells aren't always in the hands. The face and lips are common places to find tells. Records from a tournament in 1923 mention a player who wiggled his toes before throwing Rock. Tells are one reason why players study one another. Serious RPS players will spend time hunting for their tells and learning to suppress them. This can be an on-going project, because suppressing one tell can sometimes create another.

Shadowing

Another step beyond cloaking, "shadowing" is pretending to throw one thing, but changing to another at the last possible moment. This is much more difficult and requires great care in execution. Ultimately, it is up to the judges or referee to decide when that last possible moment arrives and if your hand is on the wrong throw or between throws, they are not very forgiving. There are two primary ways in which you can use shadowing. The first is to twitch your fingers during the prime merely. A hand-watching opponent may believe this to foreshadow a throw of paper or scissors, depending on which fingers you wiggle. A more advanced method of shadowing is to change the position of your hand three or four times during the last prime. This has the possibility of distracting any opponent and will likely befuddle a hand-watcher completely.

Selecting a Throw

Once the prime has started, you have to make a choice. Will it be Rock, Paper, or Scissors? This is the most discussed and debated aspect of RPS, and the foundation of your strategy. How do you decide?

Broadcasting False Tells

Of course, if you can suppress tells, you can also create them. This requires intense coordination and concentration, not to mention planning. In order to make advantageous use of a false tell, you must display the tell long enough for an opponent to notice its significance, then break the pattern at a crucial moment to score a win. Timing is everything. It won't help you to lose several points because of a false tell only to gain one when you break it.

Chaos Play

Proponents of the "Chaos School" of RPS try to select a throw randomly. An opponent cannot know what you do not know yourself. In theory, the only way to defeat a random throw is with another random throw – and then only thirty-three percent of the time. Critics of this strategy insist that there is no such thing as a random throw. Human beings will always use some impulse or inclination to choose a throw, and will therefore settle into unconscious but nonetheless predicable patterns. The Chaos School has been dwindling in recent years as tournament statistics show the greater effectiveness of other strategies.

Gambit Play

The use of Gambits in competitive RPS has been one of the greatest and most enduring breakthroughs in RPS strategy. A "Gambit" is a series of three throws used with strategic intent. "Strategic intent" in this case, means that the three throws are selected beforehand as part of a planned sequence. Selecting throws in advance helps prevent unconscious patterns from forming and can sometimes reduce tells. Choosing throws in groups of three will prevent you from switching to a purely reactive game while leaving you numerous decision-points to keep the strategy adaptable.

Beyond Gambits

The strongest criticism of Gambit play is that players still have tendencies to develop patterns. Rather than throwing Rock when angry, a Gambit player may throw Avalanche, resulting in three lost points rather than just one. The true genius of Gambit play, however, is that Gambits can be used as building blocks of larger strategies.

Chain Gambits

"Chain Gambits" are one way of expanding Gambit strategies. A Chain Gambit is a series of five throws, or two Gambits joined by a common throw. For instance, "PSPSS" is a Chain Gambit built from Scissor Sandwich and Paper Dolls. By shifting one Gambit by one throw, a Chain Gambit can prevent your opponent from obtaining multiple successive victories even if she predicts which Gambit you're using next.

Combination Moves

Gambits and Chain Gambits can also be combined to form longer, complex Combination Moves. By planning your strategy in blocks of six or more throws, you can nearly eliminate reactive tendencies. The downside of Combination Moves is that they can tax the memory. Few things are as disconcerting as forgetting your strategy half way through it.

Exclusion Strategies

"Exclusive Strategies" have been getting a lot of attention lately. An Exclusive player will at least severely limit, if not neglect altogether, the use of one of the three throws. Hence, a "Rock Exclusive" player only throws Paper and Scissors. On the surface, such a strategy seems to give an opponent a serious advantage. By neglecting Rock, a player is vulnerable to Scissors.

Many opponents, however, will focus their entire strategy on predicting when the missing throw will appear – even if it never appears at all! A few players have experimented with "Double-Exclusive Strategies," using only one throw for a whole game, but the statistics gathered so far do not indicate this is as effective as Single-Exclusion.

Meta-Strategies

"Meta-strategies" go beyond selecting your throw. In fact, in many cases, their purpose is to let you select your opponent's throw! Meta-strategies are as numerous as shells on the beach, but they are all based on one of two principles.

The first is: "If you can make your opponent believe what you want him to, you can make him behave how you want him to." This is usually accomplished through pre-game conversation or in-game banter. No one ever said RPS was played in silence!

The Meta-Predictor Strategy

In the International RoShamBo Programming Competition for Janken-playing computer algorithms, the winner was a program called Iocane powder. It used the strategy from the movie, The Princess Bride, in which the hero had to decide which cup of wine had been poisoned by his enemy. He said, "Now, a clever man would put the poison into his own goblet, because he would know that only a great fool would reach for what he was given. I am not a great fool, so I can clearly not choose the wine in front of you. But you must have known I was not a great fool. You would have counted on it, so I can clearly not choose the wine in front of me..."

It's creator, Dan Egnor argues that most people will use the same level of prediction all the time, and if you can figure out what level of prediction your opponent is operating at, it will be easy to defeat him by anticipating his moves. You will have to observe your opponent's playing style, psychology, and intelligence level to gauge their Predictor level. Few people rise above the level of single predictor however, making that a safe assumption.

Getting Under Your Opponent's Skin

The second principle of meta-strategies is: "If you can make your opponent react to you, you can play the game for her." Many players will slip into reflexive habits and strategies when angry, frustrated, afraid, or confused. If you can get your opponent into that condition, you have the control of the match.

Classic Meta-Strategies

If your opponent figures out what you're up to, meta-strategies can backfire horribly. Worse than if you'd never used them, they can leave you confused and give your opponent control of the match. A good trainer can help you create and hone new meta-strategies as well as show you when to use them and when to leave well enough alone.

Here are a few well-documented meta-strategies to use as examples or as a starting point for building your own:

Old Hat

This is one of the oldest and most well-known meta-strategies of all time. Its effectiveness is minimized by the fact that nearly every player nowadays will recognize the "Ol' 'Old Hat'" but as it is the foundation of many more developed meta-strategies, this guide would be incomplete without it.

The purpose of the "Old Hat" strategy is to demoralize an opponent into feeling inferior or intimidated. Common "Old Hat" banter may include:

"I knew that would be your next move."

"This time, actually think before you throw."

"Rock? Hmmm. . . . Frankly I am surprised that Paper obviously didn't occur to you."

"I don't suggest using the Avalanche gambit on me; I did invent it, after all."

If you can successfully frustrate, anger, or make your opponent feel inferior, you may be able to drive him into a reactive game and take control of the match.

Crystal Ball

One of the more clever meta-strategies, "Crystal Ball" is a ploy to confuse an opponent and derail what might be an otherwise effective strategy. Like "Old Hat," this is a simple and time-tested strategy that is more effective as a foundation on which to build than used in its virgin form.

To employ "Crystal Ball," tell your opponent what she is going to throw: "You're going to bring Scissors again, aren't you?"

If your opponent is unfamiliar with this ploy, you can now be certain she will not throw Scissors. That makes Paper a safe throw.

Rusty

"Rusty" is a dubious meta-strategy at best. A player using this technique will claim to be "out of practice" and predict their own defeat. This may put an opponent off her guard or instill a false sense of confidence, but this rarely has a significant effect on a match. Still, some players swear by it and continue to include it in their repertoire.

The Boy who Cried Wolf

When you're playing against someone who's highly intelligent or more experienced at Janken than you are, pretend to be a novice. They will automatically play paper to counter the perennial newbie favourite, rock and at the last minute play scissors, beating them easily. Although an effective strategy, this can only be used once or twice to a new opponent.

Benedict Arnold

This strategy involves backing down from your original plan at the last second. Start to throw paper and then suddenly pull in your fingers to form rock. This can be a costly move if not done correctly because if you are caught inbetween throws you will be considered to have lost that match.

Watch your Opponent

This strategy requires observation. Watch your opponent in matches against other people and observe his playing strategy. Challenge him to games when there are minor things to be decided and observe his playing style, so that when that really important match for who's going to pay for the beer comes up, you'll be familiar with his tactics and beat him easily.

Wildman

This is a good strategy if you are being beaten by one of the aforementioned predictor strategies. Just start throwing at random and the predictor will lose his confidence. It is useful against opponents who are more intelligent/skillful at Janken than you, but if you feel that you can out-think your opponent, the Meta Predictor is always a better strategy.

Keep your Oppoinent Surprised

It revolves around a strategy of suddenly starting the game so that your opponent has no time to think. When people are surprised, their muscles tense and once people have fallen into this cataleptic state, they will almost inevitably throw rock because they don't have time to come up with a strategy. 50-60% of people choose rock in the first round of a Janken game, even when they are not pressured, making paper a very good choice if you want to increase your chances of winning.

Probing Your Opponent

It is important to know what kind of player you are facing, their strength regarding how well they can match your abilities. Is it long-form game, a lightning round (one throw), best-of-three? In short matches, your best bet is to pick a good strategy or gambit and stick to it. In longer matches, you have the opportunity to "probe" your opponent.

Many players will develop and practice several distinct strategies. Often, after the first five or six throws, you can identify which strategy he is using. That helps you determine which of your strategies will be most helpful.

Consequently, many players develop a few opening sequences, from three throws to ten, that are independent of their larger strategies. The only purpose of these openings is to get a sense of how an opponent is going to play the match

The Backup Plan

Okay, so it's not working. She's got your strategy licked and you're dropping farther and farther behind. Don't panic! You've got a backup plan, right?

When you're down, the thing to avoid is slipping into reflexive or reactive patterns. You'll become predictable, your opponent will take control of the match, and you will lose your chance to recover the win.

A better approach is to develop and practice several independent strategies. Some techniques will work wonders against one opponent and fail miserably against the next.

It's not always easy to know when to switch tactics. Even if you lose three or four throws in a row, your opponent may still be in the dark about what you're doing. With experience and practice, though, you'll learn to tell if your opponent has you figured out.

Keeping it Varied

Finally, never stop working on your strategy! Your opponents are studying you as carefully as you're watching them. Any strategy, no matter how complicated, can be unraveled if you repeat it often enough. Change. Adapt. Replace old tactics with new approaches. Keep your game fresh, and you'll keep your opponents guessing!

THE 27 GAMBITS OF ROCK PAPER SCISSORS

A Gambit is defined as a series of three (3) successive moves made with strategic intention. Gambits became an important tool for rock, paper, scissors competitors because it helps to cancel out the possibility of the opponent guessing right what you are going to throw. It narrows your strategy to be based on every set of three throws instead of attempting to strategize on every throw. The logic behind this is to introduce more randomness by selecting among 27 options rather than only 3. Having just 3 options to choose from creates a subconscious desire to balance the three things, and the resulting pressure needed to balance can be exploited by your opponent if they are paying careful attention.

The use of Gambits in competitive RPS has been one of the most enduring and greatest breakthroughs in Rock Paper Scissors (RPS) strategy. Selecting throws in advance helps prevent unconscious patterns from forming and can sometimes reduce the subconscious signals that give away the next throw, often called "tells". Gambits form the basis of many advanced strategies and are the focal point of beginner strategy.

The Great Eight Gambits

The mathematically inclined will quickly realize that there are only twenty-seven possible Gambits. All of them have been used and documented in tournament play. Each has several names from a variety of locales. There is no such thing as a "new" Gambit. In a single game of Rock Paper Scissors with 3 rounds, there are only 27 shot combinations (Gambits). These gambits may be useful in developing your game strategy.

Rock Gambits

	THROW 1	THROW 2	THROW 3
10	ROCK	ROCK	ROCK
11	ROCK	ROCK	PAPER
12	ROCK	ROCK	SCISSORS
13	ROCK	PAPER	ROCK
14	ROCK	PAPER	PAPER
15	ROCK	PAPER	SCISSORS
16	ROCK	SCISSORS	ROCK
17	ROCK	SCISSORS	PAPER
18	ROCK	SCISSORS	SCISSORS

Paper Gambits

	THROW 1	THROW 2	THROW 3
10	PAPER	PAPER	PAPER
11	PAPER	PAPER	SCISSORS
12	PAPER	PAPER	ROCK
13	PAPER	SCISSORS	SCISSORS
14	PAPER	SCISSORS	SCISSORS
15	PAPER	SCISSORS	ROCK
16	PAPER	ROCK	SCISSORS
17	PAPER	ROCK	SCISSORS
18	PAPER	ROCK	ROCK

Scissors Gambits

	THROW 1	THROW 2	THROW 3
19	SCISSORS	SCISSORS	SCISSORS
20	SCISSORS	SCISSORS	ROCK
21	SCISSORS	SCISSORS	PAPER
22	SCISSORS	ROCK	SCISSORS
23	SCISSORS	ROCK	ROCK
24	SCISSORS	ROCK	PAPER
25	SCISSORS	PAPER	SCISSORS
26	SCISSORS	PAPER	ROCK
27	SCISSORS	PAPER	PAPER

These are the possible gambits in Rock Paper Scissors.

GAME THEORY AND ROCK PAPER SCISSORS

Game theory is a mathematical framework for analyzing cooperation and conflict. Early work was motivated by recreational and gambling games such as chess, hence the "game" in game theory. But it quickly became clear that the framework had much broader application. Today, game theory is used for mathematical modeling in a wide range of disciplines, including many of the social sciences, computer science, and evolutionary biology. In my notes, I draw examples mainly from economics.

An example: Rock-Paper-Scissors. The game Rock-Paper-Scissors (RPS) is represented in Figure 1 in what is called a game box. There are two players, 1 and 2. Each player has three strategies in the game:

	R	P	S
R	0, 0	-1, 1	1, -1
P	-1, 1	0, 0	-1, 1
S	-1, 1	1, -1	0, 0

Figure 1: A game box for Rock-Paper-Scissors (RPS).

R (rock), P (paper), and S (scissors). Player 1 is represented by the rows while player 2 is represented by the columns.

If player 1 chooses R and player 2 chooses P then this is represented as the pair, called a strategy profile, (R,P) and the result is that player 1 gets a payoff of -1 and player 2 gets a payoff of +1, represented as a payoff profile $(-1, 1)$. For interpretation, think of payoffs as encoding preferences over winning, losing, or tying, with the understanding that S beats P (because scissors cut paper), P beats R (because paper can wrap a rock . . .), and R beats S (because a rock can smash scissors). If both choose the same, then they tie. The interpretation of payoffs is actually quite delicate and I discuss this issue at length in Section 3.3. This game is called zero-sum because, for any strategy profile, the sum of payoffs is zero. In any zero-sum game, there is a number V, called the value of the game, 2 with the property that player 1 can guarantee that she gets at least V no matter what player 2 does and conversely player 2 can get $-V$ no matter what player 1 does. I provide a proof of this theorem in Section 4.5. In this particular game, $V = 0$ and both players can guarantee that they get 0 by randomizing evenly over the three strategies. Note that randomization is necessary to guarantee a payoff of at least 0. In Season 4 Episode 16 of the Simpsons, Bart persistently plays Rock against Lisa, and Lisa plays Paper, and wins. Bart here doesn't even seem to understand the game box, since he says, "Good old rock. Nothing beats that."

What is the Nash Equilibrium?

The Nash Equilibrium is a concept of game theory where the optimal outcome of a game is one where no player has an incentive to deviate from his chosen strategy after considering an opponent's choice. Overall, an individual can receive no incremental benefit from changing actions, assuming other players remain constant in their strategies. A game may have multiple Nash Equilibria or none at all.

The Nash Equilibrium is the solution to a game in which two or more players have a strategy, and with each participant considering an opponent's choice, he has no incentive, nothing to gain, by switching his strategy. In the Nash Equilibrium, each player's strategy is optimal when considering the decisions of other players. Every player wins because everyone gets the outcome they desire. To quickly test if the Nash equilibrium exists, reveal each player's strategy to the other players. If no one changes his strategy, then the Nash Equilibrium is proven.

For example, imagine a game between Tom and Sam. In this simple game, both players can choose strategy A, to receive $1, or strategy B, to lose $1. Logically, both players choose strategy A and receive a payoff of $1. If you revealed Sam's strategy to Tom and vice versa, you see that no player deviates from the original choice. Knowing the other player's move means little and doesn't change either player's behavior. The outcome A, A represents a Nash Equilibrium.

Pure-Strategy Nash Equilibrium Rational players think about actions that the other players might take. In other words, players form beliefs about one another's behavior. For example, in the BoS game, if the man believed the woman would go to the ballet, it would be prudent for him to go to the ballet as well. Conversely, if he believed that the woman would go to the fight, it is probably best if he went to the fight as well. So, to maximize his payoff, he would select the strategy that yields the greatest expected payoff given his belief. Such a strategy is called a best response (or best reply).

Suppose player i has some belief $s_{-i} \in S_{-i}$ about the strategies played by the other players. Player i's strategy $s_i \in S_i$ is a best response if

$$u_i(s_i, s_{-i}) \geq u_i(s_i, s_{-i}) \text{ for every } s_i \in S_i.$$

We now define the best response correspondence), $BR_i(s_{-i})$, as the set of best responses player i has to s_{-i}. It is important to note that the best response correspondence is setvalued. That is, there may be more than one best response for any given belief of player i. If the other players stick to s_{-i}, then player i can do no better than using any of the strategies in the set $BR_i(s_{-i})$.

In the BoS game, the set consists of a single member:

BRm(F) = {F} and BRm(B) = {B}.

Thus, here the players have a single optimal strategy for every belief.

In this game, BR1(L) = {M}, BR1(C) = {U,M}, and BR1(R) = {U}.

Also, BR2(U) = {C,R}, BR2(M) = {R}, and BR2(D) = {C}.

You should get used to thinking of the best response correspondence as a set of strategies, one for each combination of the other players' strategies. (This is why we enclose the values of the correspondence in braces even when there is only one element.)

Player 2

	L	C	R
U	2, 2	1, 4	4, 4
M	3, 3	1, 0	1, 5
D	1, 1	0, 5	2, 3

Player 1

Figure 2: The Best Response Game.

We can now use the concept of best responses to define Nash equilibrium: a Nash equilibrium is a strategy profile such that each player's strategy is a best response to the other players' strategies:

The strategy profile $(s* i, s* -i) \in S$ is a pure-strategy Nash equilibrium if, and only if $s* i \in BRi(s* -i)$ for each player

$i \in I$. An equivalent useful way of defining Nash equilibrium is in terms of the payoffs players receive from various strategy profiles.

Rock Paper Scissors and Game Theory

On the count of three and the verbal command "shoot", each player simultaneously forms his hand into the shape of either a rock, a piece of paper, or a pair of scissors. If both pick the same shape, the game ends in a tie. Otherwise, one player wins and the other loses according to the following rule: rock beats scissors, scissors beats paper, and paper beats rock. Each obtains a payoff of 1 if he wins, −1 if he loses, and 0 if he ties.

Figure 3:

Rock, Paper, Scissors.

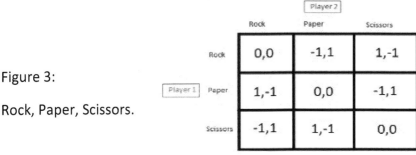

It is immediately obvious that this game has no Nash equilibrium in pure strategies: The player who loses or ties can always switch to another strategy and win. This game is symmetric, and we shall look for symmetric mixed strategy equilibria first. Let p, q, and $1 - p - q$ be the probability that a player chooses R, P, and S respectively. We first argue that we must look only at completely mixed strategies (that is, mixed strategies that put a positive probability on every available pure strategy). Suppose not, so p1 = 0 in some (possibly asymmetric) MSNE. If player 1 never chooses R, then playing P is strictly dominated by S for player 2, so she will play either R or S. However, if player 2 never chooses P, then S is strictly dominated by R for player 1, so player 1 will choose either R or P in equilibrium. However, since player 1 never chooses R, it follows that he must choose P with probability 1. But in this case player 2's optimal strategy will be to play S, to which either R or S are better choices than P. Therefore, p1 = 0 cannot occur in equilibrium. Similar arguments establish that in any equilibrium, any strategy must be completely mixed. We now look for a symmetric equilibrium. Player 1's payoff from R is $p(0) + q(-1) + (1 - p - q)(1) = 1 - p - 2q$. His payoff from P is $2p + q - 1$. His payoff from S is $q - p$. In an MSNE, the payoffs from all three pure strategies must be the same, so:

$$1 - p - 2q = 2p + q - 1 = q - p$$

Solving these equalities yields p = q = 1/3.

Whenever player 2 plays the three pure strategies with equal probability, player 1 is indifferent between his pure strategies, and hence can play any mixture. In particular, he can play the same mixture as player 2, which would leave player 2 indifferent among his pure strategies. This verifies the first condition in Proposition 1. Because these strategies are completely mixed, we are done. Each player's strategy in the symmetric Nash equilibrium is (1/3, 1/3, 1/3). That is, each player chooses among his three actions with equal probabilities. Is this the only MSNE? We already know that any mixed strategy profile must consist only of completely mixed strategies in equilibrium. Arguing in a way similar to that for the pure strategies, we can show that there can be no equilibrium in which players put different weights on their pure strategies. You should check for MSNE in all combinations. That is, you should check whether there are equilibria, in which one player chooses a pure strategy and the other mixes; equilibria, in which both mix; and equilibria in which neither mixes. Note that the mixtures need not be over the entire strategy spaces, which means you should check every possible subset. Thus, in a 2×2 two-player game, each player has three possible choices: two in pure strategies and one that mixes between them. This yields 9 total combinations to check. Similarly, in a 3 × 3 two-player game, each player has 7 choices: three pure strategies, one completely mixed, and three partially mixed. This means that we must examine 49 combinations! (You can see how this can quickly get out of hand.) Note that in this case, you must check both conditions of Proposition 1.

We have established that Rock Paper Scissors does not have a dominant strategy for either of the players. How do you use that information to incur that there is no Nash equilibrium? Quite simple! If Player 2's strategy is Rock, Player 1 should choose Paper, but if Player 1 chooses Paper, it is profitable for Player 2 to deviate and choose Scissors instead. When player 2 chooses Scissors, Player 1 would want to deviate and choose Rock, and so forth. Thus, we can see that there is no Nash Equilibrium for this game owing to the cyclical manner of the game.

Game Theory in Rock Paper Scissors Lizard Spock

Again this game has no Nash Equilibrium. The Rock Paper Scissors interplay remains the same as the classical game. The only changes are two more alternative actions have been added, that of Lizard and Spock. The link established using them is again cyclical in nature allowing no strategy to dominate the others. This extended version manages to preserve the randomness of the outcome of the game and keeps it as a game of chance.

THE PSYCOLOGY OF ROCK PAPER SCISSORS

Many people may have thought that RPS was similar to flipping coins or throwing dice—a useful method to choose something at random. However, there's far more to the game than meets the eye. RPS involves

observation, mindfulness, manipulation, emotional intelligence, strategy, and skill. And some of that skill involves exploiting your opponent's non-random behavior.

If people were truly playing RPS in random fashion, it would be impossible to employ any strategy. You would do best to just choose your weapon at random. Eventually, you would have an equal likelihood of winning, losing, or tying. Several small-scale experiments have confirmed this strategy—where every player chooses the three actions with equal probability in each round—often seems to be in effect.

Then a study out of China by Zhijian Wang at Zhejiang University suggested that RPS is actually a game of psychology more than chance, thus making it possible to exploit your opponent's predictable patterns. Zhijian and colleagues looked at 360 students divided into 60 groups. In each group, the players played 300 rounds of RPS against each other. The winners were paid in proportion to the number of their victories.

On the surface, the results of the study appeared to be no surprise: The players in all the groups chose each action about one-third of the time—just as if it was random. But taking a closer look at their behavior uncovers a strategy called "conditional response," or what turns out to be a "win-stay, lose-shift" strategy. These findings inspire further questions as to whether this conditional response is a hard-wired neural mechanism or a learned process intrinsic in basic decision-making. When players try to employ some kind of strategy, they decrease the chances that the game will remain random.

Here are psychological strategies employed by RPS aficionados to use against non-random opponents.Winners tend to stick with the same action that led to their success. We repeat what works. So, if you lose with rock (they played paper), they'll play with paper again next and you should go with scissors. In other words, when you lose, jump ahead two actions in the sequence.Losers change their strategy and move to the next action (clockwise: R – P – S) in the sequence. If they lose with rock (you played paper), they'll play paper next. So you should play scissors. In other words, when you win, go to the next action in the sequence.

Know the symbols. There may be subliminal reasons for your opponent choosing a particular symbol.

Rock: Very aggressive, symbolized by the fist. Players subconsciously think of rock as a weapon and will rely on it when other strategies are not working.

Scissors: Some aggression, as they are sharp and dangerous, but also useful craft tools. Represent controlled aggression used as a clever throw— often when someone is confident or winning.

Paper: The most subtle move. An open hand is passive, peaceful, and friendly. Some players won't use this when falling behind because it may symbolize weakness. Other players identify paper with writing and as such, the power of print is a subtle attack. In those cases, paper may be used to signify superiority.

As in a chess match, you must think ahead. Against a more seasoned opponent, they will purposefully not begin with rock, which is too obvious. They may consider you to be a novice, expect rock and will therefore open with paper. Against a veteran, you should lead with scissors: at worst, you'll tie.

Manipulation

Gently manipulate your opponent toward choosing a particular action, or not choosing a particular action. If you can subtly get your opponent to not throw rock, then you choose scissors (leads to either a tie or a win). Manipulation comes in many flavors—How to win friends and influence people…Tell your opponent what you are going to throw and then actually do it. As they will likely not expect you to be that fearless and honest, the one thing that they probably won't throw down is the action that beats yours. If you say, "rock", your opponent will likely throw rock or scissors, leading to your victory or tie. Another subtle manipulation technique derives from neurolinguistic programming. At the start of the game, remind someone about the rules. You might say, "Scissors beats paper, paper beats rock (show a sample of

the rock with arm movement), and rock crushes scissors" (demonstrate how the rock crushes the scissors). In magic, this is called a "force." Now expect them to throw down a rock. Obviously, you'll answer with paper.

No one likes to be predictable. If someone has already thrown a double (typically because they won the first time with it), they are very unlikely to use it for a third time. If they used scissor twice, their next move will either be rock or paper. Paper is your best move to either win or tie. If they do two rocks, you follow with scissors. Two papers, you answer with rock.

Know the Stats

Statistically, the expected average is 33.3% if everything is completely random. it turns out that all things are not equal in Rock Paper Scissors and choosing paper a little more frequently may give you a very slight advantage.

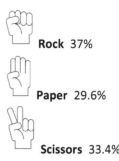

Rock 37%

Paper 29.6%

Scissors 33.4%

Observe your opponent's hands before he throws. A tight hand when raised often ends in a rock. A loose hand becomes a paper and the first two fingers loose results in a scissors. Closely observe your opponent as he or she plays RPS against others, do they tend to fall back on one particular throw? Is there a pattern? Do they telegraph their throw by moving their fingers early?

As a result of RPS contests, many complex algorithms have been developed with heuristically designed strategies, sub-strategies and metastrategies based on past performances, frequency analysis, history matching, multi-history matching, and even random guessing. Of course, if you were fortunate enough to have very keen observational skills and lightening fast reflexes, you'd have an amazing advantage. When the robot hand from the University of Tokyo plays RPS, it uses a high-speed camera to recognize within one msec. which shape the human hand is making, and delivers the winning shape 100% of the time.

Rock Paper Scissors, often thought of as a game of random chance, may not be so random after all. According to a study published in Nature and recently reported on by Discover, most humans have a tendency to make moves that are irrational, unconscious, and to some degree, predictable.

In a previous study, researchers pitted students against each other in 300 games of rock paper scissors and found that players had a tendency to replay winning moves and upgrade losing moves (for instance, switching from paper to scissors after a loss).

This new study took a slightly different approach. The researchers, led by Benjamin James Dyson, pitted players against a computer. Their findings not only backed up the ideas from the previous study, but they showed that human players had a slight preference for rock.

As in the previous study, participants had a tendency to stick with winning moves and switch in the case of a loss or a draw, according to Discover. However, while the initial study analyzed the kinds of moves humans make against humans—a situation in which moves were made with some form of bias on each side—this study looked at the interactions between humans and computers. That is, participants in the previous study might have realized their competitors were playing non-randomly and tried to pick up on their patterns of play, thus altering the moves that were made. In the Nature study, however, humans likely believed the computer was making random moves—and yet, they still employed the same unconscious strategies.

Researchers believe the study may have implications outside the realm of a simple game of rock-paper-scissors. In fact, they explain that this form of unconscious, irrational decision-making could have an impact on other higher stakes situations.

"Rock, Paper, Scissors (RPS) represents a unique gaming space in which the predictions of human rational decision-making can be compared with actual performance," the study explains. "The data reveal the strategic vulnerability of individuals following the experience of negative rather than positive outcome, the tensions between behavioural and cognitive influences on decision making, and underline the dangers of increased behavioural predictability in other recursive, non-cooperative environments such as economics and politics.

ROCK PAPER SCISSORS
TOURNAMENTS AND ETIQUETTE

Ever wanted to compete on a larger stage, maybe you think you are outgrowing your own community and want to go Pro. Then Rock Paper Scissors Tournaments are an important chapter for you. There are a lot of such tournaments where people are competing with the classical game of rock paper scissors and the winner gets a cash awards. Started in 2009 Japan has an annual tournament held by AKB48 a popular Japanese Girl Group. This event has players cheering, crying and jumping from happiness. The winner of this tournament is named the Janken Queen.

The tournaments are not held only in Japan, but also in the other countries and cities, like Las Vegas, UK and the other places. The competitions that are held in Japan are not held there for the first time and are very intense. In Japan the paper rock scissors tournaments are a daily thing that is held almost every morning. It is one of the most popular shows in the country where the celebrities are also participating at the competitions and the viewers can watch them on the screens.

Many tournaments have dissapreared over time. There was a national competition league in USA held by the now defunct USARPS this tournament was held in 2006 and 2007 in Las Vegas. The champion was given a prize of $50,000. The now defunct World RPS Society held annual tournaments from 2006-2009. The winner of this tournament won $10,000. This event was held in Toronto, Canada.

In the UK there is currently an Annual Rock Paper Scissors Tournament. It is run by Wacky Nation. This event started in 2014 and has been running every year since. It last 3 hours and the winner receives $100, a bottle of champers, a trophy and tremendous respect and bragging rights.

What are the rules of the games?

The rules at the tournament are pretty simple and the players need to stand at each side of the table. There is also a referee that is guiding the game and giving yellow or red cards if some of the players are not behaving well. At the beginning of the game the players shake their hands, count 1 and 2 and then on the 3rd count their throw the move. The rock beats the scissors, the paper beats the rock and the scissors beat the paper. No moves like lizard, spock, rain or grenade are not going to be recognized by the referee. The players plan to confuse their opponents with announcing or giving a hint about their next move, with taunts, and costumes. In the last minutes the games can get very tense, so you better get prepared for the end.

RPS is a decision making game of speed, strategy, wits, and dexterity between players who could not arrive at a decision using other means. There is an agreement between the players that the result of the game is accepted to be binding. The game is played by substituting the elements of Rock, Paper, and Scissors with standard hand signals.

Set-Up: Players should enter the game area with an intent to play. Players should come to their match prepared with knowledge of the general rules of play.

Spacing: Opponents shall give adequate spacing to allow their opponent a comfortable throw. The ideal spacing during tournament play is from 2 feet – 3 feet.

Priming: Opponents shall maintain an adequate speed while priming their throw. Opponents will mirror earhother. If a player feels like their opponent is going too quickly or slowly they have the right to appeal to the referee.

Note: At the conclusion of the match after the winner has been determined, some players will offer a vertical paper throw or "handshake". While this gesture is seen in other circles as good manners to thank your opponent for the match, it is important to note that this action should not be expected or required in RPS, due to the fact that in general a "Handshake" is used as "deal sealer" between two parties. Since the results of an RPS match are considered to be binding, the "handshake" can be considered a redundancy since, in effect, the " deal" has already been "sealed" with the outcome of the match.

THE GREATEST GAMES OF
ROCK PAPER SCISSORS

Because of Rock Paper Scissors' worldwide popularity there are many instances which could be considered some of the greatest games of rock paper scissors. There have been many great games documented in television in shows such as, The Simpsons, Sienfeld, That 70's Show and Southpark. In these instances Rock Paper Scissors has been used to one characters incompetence.

The greatest games of Rock Paper Scissors are a precident setting way of using RPS to help settle disputes in a legal matter. The other was a $20,000,000 USD game of Rock Paper Scissors.

Rock Paper Scissors in an American Legal Trail

In 2006, American federal judge Gregory Presnell from the Middle District of Florida ordered opposing sides play a game of Rock Paper Scissors in order to settle where the two lawyers would conduct the deposition of a witness. The choices were the building where they both work, four floors apart, or a court reporter's office down the street. The ruling in Avista Management v. Wausau Underwriters stated:

Upon consideration of the Motion – the latest in a series of Gordian knots that the parties have been unable to untangle without enlistlng the assistance of the federal courts – it is ORDERED that said Motion is DENIED. Instead, the Court will fashion a new form of alternative dispute resolution, to wit: at 4:00 P.M. on Friday, June 30, 2006, counsel shall convene at a neutral site agreeable to both parties. If counsel cannot agree on a neutral site, they shall meet on the front steps of the Sam M. Gibbons U.S. Courthouse, 801 North Florida Ave., Tampa, Florida 33602. Each lawyer shall be entitled to be accompanied by one paralegal who shall act as an attendant and witness. At that time and location, counsel shall engage in one (1) game of "rock, paper, scissors." The winner of this engagement shall be entitled to select the location for the 30(b)(6) deposition to be held somewhere in Hillsborough County during the period July 11–12, 2006.

Unfortunalty, the lawyers were able to come to a conclusion over where the deposition was held without the game being playe, but the fact that now there is precident in the legal system to use Rock Paper Scissors to settle disputes it is the greatest game that never was.

The Auction House Rock Paper Scissors Match

In 2005, when Takashi Hashiyama, CEO of Japanese television equipment manufacturer Maspro Denkoh, decided to auction off the collection of Impressionist paintings owned by his corporation, including works by Paul Cézanne, Pablo Picasso, and Vincent van Gogh, he contacted two leading auction houses, Christie's International and Sotheby's Holdings, seeking their proposals on how they would bring the collection to the market as well as how they would maximize the profits from the sale. Both firms made elaborate proposals, but neither was persuasive enough to get Hashiyama's business. Unwilling to split up the collection into separate auctions, Hashiyama asked the firms to decide between themselves who would hold the auction, which included Cézanne's Large Trees Under the Jas de Bouffan, worth $12–16 million.

The houses were unable to reach a decision. Hashiyama told the two firms to play rock–paper–scissors to decide who would get the rights to the auction, explaining that "it probably looks strange to others, but I believe this is the best way to decide between two things which are equally good".

The auction houses had a weekend to come up with a choice of move. Christie's went to the 11-year-old twin daughters (Flora and Alice) of the international director of Christie's Impressionist and Modern Art Department Nicholas Maclean, who suggested "scissors" because "Everybody expects you to choose 'rock'."

"Everybody knows you always start with scissors," she added. "Rock is way too obvious, and scissors beats paper." Flora piped in. "Since they were beginners, scissors was definitely the safest," she said, adding that if the other side were also to choose scissors and another round was required, the correct play would be to stick to scissors -- because, as Alice explained, "Everybody expects you to choose rock."

Sotheby's said that they treated it as a game of chance and had no particular strategy for the game, but went with "paper".

The centerpiece of the company's collection, Paul Cezanne's "Les grands arbres au Jas de Bouffan," sold for $11.8 million. Alfred Sisley piece, "La manufacture de Sevres," sold for $1.6 million. Pablo Picasso's "Boulevard de Clichy" went for $1.7 million, and Vincent van Gogh's "Vue de la chambre de l'artiste, rue Lepic" went for $2.7 million.

How much did Christie's make off this single game of Rock Paper Scissors? Christie's charges a premium of 20% on the first $200,000 and 12% on the rest. In the end they made 2.2 million by choosing scissors. I hope the twins were able to get some toys for their decision.

DIFFERENT VARIATIONS OF
ROCK PAPER SCISSORS

Players have developed numerous cultural and personal variations on the game, from simply playing the same game with different objects, to expanding into more weapons and rules.

A multiple player variations can be played: Players stand in a circle and all throw at once. If rock, paper, and scissors are all thrown, it is a stalemate, and they rethrow. If only two throws are present, all players with the losing throw are eliminated. Play continues until only the winner remains.

Different weapons

In the Malaysian version of the game, "scissors" is replaced by "bird," represented with the finger tips of five fingers brought together to form a beak. The open palm represents water. Bird beats water (by drinking it); stone beats bird (by hitting it), and stone loses to water (because it sinks in it).

Singapore also has a related hand-game called "ji gu pa," where "ji" refers to the bird gesture, "gu" refers to the stone gesture, and "pa" refers to the water gesture. The game is played by two players using both hands. At the same time, they both say, ji gu pa!" At "pa!" they both show two open-palmed hands. One player then changes his hand gestures while calling his new combination out (e.g., "pa gu!"). At the same time, the other player changes his hand gestures as well. If one of his hand gestures is the same as the other one, that hand is "out, " and he puts it behind his back; he is no longer able to play that hand for the rest of the round. The players take turns in this fashion until one player loses by having both hands sent "out." "Ji gu pa" is most likely a transcription of the Japanese names for the different hand gestures in the original jan-ken game, "choki" (scissors), "guu" (rock) and "paa" (paper).

In Japan, a "strip-poker" variant of rock-paper-scissors is known as (Yakyuken). The loser of each round removes an article of clothing. The game is a minor part of porn culture in Japan, and other Asian countries after the influence of TV variety shows and Soft On Demand.

Using the same tripartite division, there is a full-body variation instead of the hand signs called "Bear, Hunter, Ninja". In this iteration the participants stand back-to-back and at the count of three (or ro-sham-bo as is traditional) turn around facing each other using their arms evoking one of the totems. The players' choices break down as: Hunter shoots bear; Bear eats ninja; Ninja kills the hunter. The game was popularized with a FedEx commercial where warehouse employees had too much free time on their hands.

In the British comedy show I'm Sorry I Haven't a Clue, variations on this are done like Glass, Pudding, Cat and Cow, Lake, Bomb, with similar logic.

Additional weapons

As long as the number of moves is an odd number and each move defeats exactly half of the other moves while being defeated by the other half, any combination of moves will function as a game. For example, 5-, 7-, 9-, 11-, 15-, 25-, and 101-weapon versions exist. Adding new gestures has the effect of reducing the odds of a tie while increasing the complexity of the game. The probability of a tie in an odd-number-of-weapons game can be calculated based on the number of weapons n as $1/n$, so the probability of a tie is $1/3$ in standard rock-paper-scissors, but $1/5$ in a version that offered five moves instead of three.

Similarly, the French game "pierre, papier, ciseaux, puits" (stone, paper, scissors, well) is unbalanced; both the stone and scissors fall into the well and lose to it, while paper covers both stone and well. This means two "weapons," well and paper can defeat two moves, while the other two weapons each defeats only one of the other three choices. The rock has no advantage to well, so optimal strategy is to play paper-scissors-well. This version is also played in some areas of Germany; it often adds "the bull" (which drinks the well empty, eats the paper, but gets stabbed by the scissors, and is crushed by the rock). The well is made by forming a circle with the thumb and index finger to show the opening of a stone well; the bull is made by making a fist but extending the little finger and index finger to show the bull's horns. In theory, "unbalanced" games are less random but more psychological, more closely resembling real world conflicts. However, games of this sort are popular more for novelty than for exploring such ideas.

Rock Paper Scissors Lizard Spock

One popular five-weapon expansion is "rock-paper-scissors-Spock-lizard," invented by Sam Kass and Karen Bryla, which adds "Spock" and "lizard" to the standard three choices. "Spock" is signified with the Star TrekVulcan salute, while "lizard" is shown by forming the hand into a sock-puppet-like mouth. Spock smashes scissors and vaporizes rock; he is poisoned by a lizard and disproven by paper. Lizard poisons Spock and eats paper; it is crushed by rock and decapitated by scissors. This variant was mentioned in a 2005 article in The Times of London and was later the subject of an episode of the American sitcom The Big Bang Theory in 2008 (as rock-paper-scissors-lizard-Spock).

Spock

Lizard

The majority of such proposed generalizations are isomorphic to a simple game of modular arithmetic, where half the differences are wins for player one. For instance, rock-paper-scissors-Spock-lizard (note the different order of the last two moves) may be modeled as a game in which each player picks a number from one to five. Subtract the number chosen by player two from the number chosen by player one, and then take the remainder modulo 5 of the result. Player one is the victor if the difference is one or three, and player two is the victor if the difference is two or four. If the difference is zero, the game is a tie.

Alternatively, the rankings in rock-paper-scissors-Spock-lizard may be modeled by a comparison of the parity of the two choices. If it is the same (two odd-numbered moves or two even-numbered ones), then the lower number wins, while if they are different (one odd and one even) the higher wins. Using this algorithm, additional moves can easily be added two at a time while keeping the game balanced.

Playing Rock Paper Scissors using Legs

Rock Paper Scissors can also be played using players' legs: legs together mean "rock," legs spread means "paper," and one leg back and one leg forward is "scissors." This style is often combined with a word game in which players must say words for rock, paper and scissors.

Human Rock Paper Scissors

Human Rock Paper Scissors is a fun, quick ice-breaker that can be used for a medium-sized group of people. Many are familiar with the classic hand game, rock-paper-scissors, each of which conquers one another depending on the combination. This game is a play on the game but requires people to get on their feet, move, and act as a team, rather than an individual.

This ice-breaker is especially fun because it can be tailored to many different themes and variations.

Setup: As a large group, decide a full-body pose that will signify each element (e.g. Rock – each person of one group will bend down and hug their knees and curl into a ball. So they look like a rock, Scissors – each person of one group will stand with legs shoulder-width apart and both arms up and hands behind the head, so they look like a scissor).

Playing: After the poses are decided, break participants into two groups. For each round, each group will need to do one of the poses (everyone in each group will need to do the same pose). Each group will have 5 minutes to strategize. Once all of the groups have their poses ready, a facilitator will have the two groups face each other and count down from three (e.g. three….two…one….SHOOT). On "SHOOT" each group will need to strike one of the three poses. Rock beats Scissors, Scissors beat Paper, and Paper beats Rock. You can play however times you'd like. Best out of 5 rounds is a good number for a medium sized group.

If you want to try some different themes of this game you can try some of the following themes or make up some of your own!

Lord of the Rings: Hobbit, Elf, Orc (Orc beats Hobbit, Elf beats Orc, Hobbit beats Elf)

Schools: Stanford, Cal, USC (Stanford beats USC, Cal beats Stanford, USC beats Cal)

Super Heroes: Batman, Spiderman, Green Lantern (Spiderman beats Batman, Batman beats Green Lantern, Green Lantern beats Spiderman)

Disney Villains: Maleficent, Ursula, Jafar (Maleficent beats Ursula, Ursula beats Jafar, Jafar beats Maleficent)

ROCK PAPER SCISSORS
IN DIFFERENT PARTS OF THE WORLD

Rock Paper Scissors in Japan

The Japanese version of Rock Paper Scissors is known as Janken, Japanese have taken Janken to a higher level regarding its usage and what it means to them in their daily life engagements. It is so significant that in Japan Janken is used to settle an argument between two persons who have divergent opinions on a matter, anyone who wins is considered to have won the argument. Janken is popular among Japanese children that they employ it in deciding between two options; whoever wins the game has his or her choice adopted. Japanese children will play janken tens if not hundreds of times a day, so it's important to know about janken if you're going to be teaching in schools.

In Japan, janken dates from the 17th century and is an evolution of an older game that was imported from China that dates from 200BC! Japan, however, is often credited with helping Rock Paper Scissors spread through the West. Various forms of janken exist all over Japan. The phrases and sometimes the hand gestures can vary from region to region. Ask a child to teach you their swag. The version described below is the most common. The good news is that the rules and gestures are the same as in English. Scissors beats paper; rock beats scissors, paper beats rock. Rock is called "Guu." Paper is called "Paa." Scissors is called "Choki." Paper is called "Paa."

To get the game started, players shout together "Saisho wa guu" (Starting with stone) and pump their fists in time. This is quickly followed by "Janken pon!" and on "pon" both players show their hands in front of them, displaying "Guu," "Choki" or "Paa." If there is a draw, both players chant (nihongo)"Aiko desho!", and on the "sho!" both players show their hands again.

But what's the point of having a Paper Rock Scissors competition for idols? It's two-fold. First, it's another big event for AKB48 groups and their fans, and second, a paper rock scissors tournament is a rather cutesy, especially when it's taken so seriously. Competitors cosplay, there's a ref, and even if your favorite idol loses, you can cheer her on in the wake of defeat. However, the reason why the winning idol freaks out is that this year the tournament champ gets a to be the center (main idol) in a special spin-off group.

In the hyper-competitive world of Japanese idols, that is quite a prize! It's also a way for group members, who might not yet have a large following, to have a moment in the spotlight. This isn't the first paper-rock-scissors tournament in Japan. In the past, Japanese variety shows have held janken competitions, but they certainly were not this intense. Such competitions are not in Japan only. All this might seem rather peculiar in the West, but in Japan, paper-rock-scissors is a daily thing; every morning on one of the country's most popular morning shows, celebrities challenge viewers to rock-paper-scissors matches, and viewers can even track their wins!

In the janken game, parted index and middle finger mean "scissors," fist means "rock," and an open hand means "paper." The basic rule is that scissors cut paper, rocks break scissors, and paper wraps rock. For example, if one player shows parted fingers (scissors) and the other shows an open hand (paper), the one showing scissors wins. Whenever they start to play, players says out loud "Jan-ken-pon!" in short, or "Jan-ken-pon, aiko de sho!" in a longer phrase. Usually, when playing janken, there is the need for one person to be the leader, with any number of additional players (not limited to two people as in the usual rock-scissors-paper game). Another way to play janken is that players who do not show the same hand as the leader, no matter what it is, loses.

Guriko, is another game which uses our hands to play janken, and stairs as the "start-finish" path. The rules of janken are similar, but all players should start from the bottom or the beginning of the stairway. Next, if one wins with rock (gu-ri-ko), he can advance three steps because guriko is written with three characters. If he wins with scissors (cho-ko-re-to) or with paper (pai-na-pu-ru), he can climb six steps because both are written using six characters. The one to reach the top of the stairs first is the winner.

Rock Paper Scissors in Korea

The western order of saying these three words when playing the game of the same name is: Rock Paper Scissors, however, it goes Scissors, Rock, Paper when it is said in Korean.

There are two ways;

Muk Jji Ppa: Muk is rock, Jji is scissors, Ppa is paper. First, they say, Muk Jji Ppa, show their shape on Ppa and the person who wins now must try to match the other person's shape. So again they say Muk Jji Ppa and both players change their shape. The winner wants the two to be the same; the loser wants his/her shape to be different from the other player. If they are different, then the next turn is based on what shapes the players are holding after they tried to match/not match. If Player 1 won with Muk and Player 2 lost with Jji, and Player 1 changed to Jji but Player 2 changed to Muk, then Player 2 tries to match because his/her shape won. The process continues until the loser matches with the winner.

Gawi Bawi Bo: This a more traditional game to Rock Paper Scissors, everything is the same, but for scissors, there are 3 types; gun-type scissors, normal scissors, and chibi scissors.

Normal ones: The normal ones are those scissors with index and middle fingers.

Gun ones: These are thumb and index fingers.

Chibi ones: These are ring finger and pinky. However, you have to say "Gawi Bawi Bo" when you show your pick

Rock Paper Scissors in France

France also has Rock, Paper, Scissors somewhat similar to Austria's. The French style is as follows; It involves four shapes of hands instead of three. The rock is same as the Japanese Goo and same as the Austrian style; like a cylinder. Leaf, same as Japanese Pa, opening all the fingers, which is different from the Austrian style. Scissors, same as Japanese Choki, showing index finger and middle finger.

Who beats who? Well beats Rock and Scissors, because both of them sink in the well. Scissors beats Leaf because it can cut leaves. Leaf beats Well by covering it and beats Rock by wrapping it up. Rock beats Scissors by dulling the metal. The French paly the game to kill time.

Rock Paper Scissors in Spain

The game "rock, paper, scissors" is played all over the Spanish-speaking world. In most countries, it is Piedra – rock, papel – paper, o tijera -or scissors. (In Peru it is called janquenpón, from the Japanese yan-ken-pon, and in Chile, it is called cachipún). Teach your child to play this simple game in Spanish. The actions reinforce the meaning of the Spanish words. Also, rhythm aids pronunciation. It is a great way to use Spanish with your child!

Rock Paper Scissors in China

In Shanghai, they say "cei dong li a cei" when playing rock-paper-scissor. Where "cei" means "guess," rock-paper-scissor in China evolved from a more ancient game which was originally called "guess fist." "Guess fist" is often played as a drinking game. In the early days (before Ming dynasty), the game involved guessing items held in another person's hand. Later it evolved into guessing the sum of fingers that two people playing the game will show (which may still be popular in some Chinese regions, and people say auspicious phrases associated with each number when guessing instead of just saying the number).

Rock Paper Scissors in the Philippines

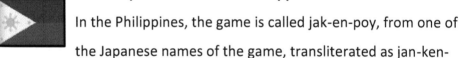

In the Philippines, the game is called jak-en-poy, from one of the Japanese names of the game, transliterated as jan-ken-pon. In a longer version of the game, a four-line song is sung, with hand gestures displayed at the end of each (or the final) line: "Jack-en-poy! / Hali-hali-hoy! / Sino'ng matalo, / siya'ng unggoy!" ("Jack-en-poy! / Hali-hali-hoy! / Whoever loses is the monkey!") In the former case, the person with the most wins at the end of the song wins the game. A shorter version of the game uses the chant "Bato-bato-pick" ("Rock-rock-pick [i.e. choose]") instead.

Rock Paper Scissors in Austria

In Austria, instead of throwing a rock, the competitors use a Well. They connect their thumb with their fingers to form a shape like a cylinder with an open hole in the well. The rules for this game are paper floats in a well, Scissors sink in the Well and of course Scissors custs paper.

Rock Paper Scissors Gameplay and Names across the World

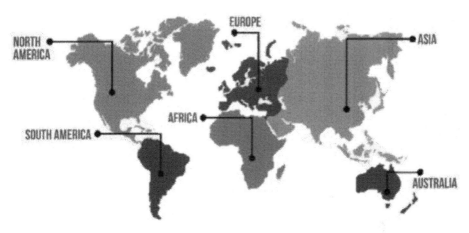

We have compiled the different throws used across the world and the different names used for our great game. We have sorted them according to the various continents. We have grouped some countries in Asia to nearby continents do to the number of different countries with different names for Rock Paper Scissors. All hand games that feature 4 elements and above have been omitted.

The Different Names for RPS in the Americas

Canada: Ro Sham Bo, Roche Ciseaux Papier, Bear Ninja Gun

USA: Ro Sham Bo, Jan Ken Po, Fargling, Bear Ninja Gun

South America: Piedra, Papel o Tijeras

The Different Names for RPS in Europe

France: Ro Sham Bo, Pierre Feuille Ciseaux

Germany: Schere Stein Papier, Shnick Shnack Shnuck, Klick Klack Kluck, Stein schleift Schere, Schnibbeln, Knobeln oder Schniekern

UK: Chinging, Paper Scissors Stone, Paper Scissors Rock

The Different Names for RPS in Australia

Australia: Paper, Scissors Rock, Rock Scissors Paper

New Zealand: Paper Scissors Rock

The Different Names for RPS in Africa

South Africa: Ching Chong Chow

The Different Names for RPS in Asia

China: Shoushiling, Jiandao Shítou Bu, Tsay Deng Qiang, Cei Dong li a Cei, Jing Gang Chui, Ding Gang Chui

Indonesia: Muk Chi Baa, Elephant Human Ant

Korea: Gawi Bawi Bo, Kai Bai Bo, Muk Chi Baa, Muk Jji Ppa

Singapore: Stone Dragon Water

Vietnam: One Two Three, Hammer Nail Paper, Hammer Scissors Paper

Myanmar: General, Gun, Hands Raised

Malasyia: Rock Bud Well, Rock Beak Well

Japan: Janken, Jan Ken Pon, Guu Choki Paa

Thailand: Janji

Phillipenes: Jak en Poy

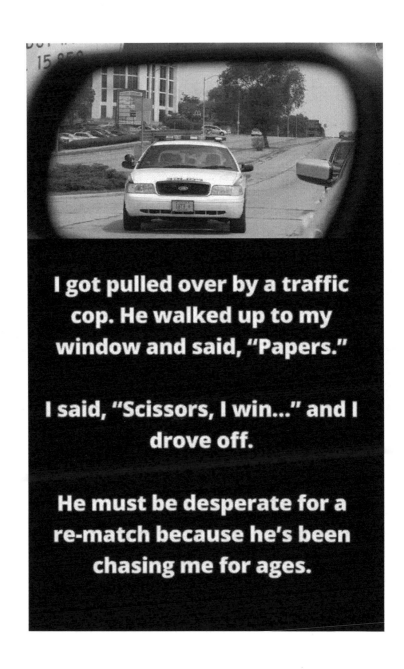

I got pulled over by a traffic cop. He walked up to my window and said, "Papers."

I said, "Scissors, I win..." and I drove off.

He must be desperate for a re-match because he's been chasing me for ages.

Before paper and scissors

lizclimo.tumblr.com

ROCK PAPER SCISSORS JOKES

I understand that Scissors can beat Paper, and I get how Rock can beat Scissors, but thers's no way Paper can beat Rock. Paper is supposed to magically wrap around Rock leaving it immobile? Why can't paper do this to scissors? Screw scissors, why can't paper do this to people? Why isin't notebook paper constantly suffocating students while they take notes in class? I'll tell you why: because paper can't beat anybody; a rock would tear it up in 2 seconds. When I play rock paper scissors, I always choose rock. Then when somebody claims to beat me with their paper I can punch them in the face with my already clenched fist and say, "Oh shoot, I'm sorry. I thought paper would protect you!"

Joke by Unknown

I hate when I go in for a traditional handshake and the other person comes in with the fist thing. Then I need to scamble, oh were doing the fists, ok, I guess since yours is newer were doing your thing. So I don't do it, I just go Paper covers Rock!

I like two thirds of rock paper scissors. Rock breaks scissors: these scissors are bent, they're destroyed, I can't cut stuff - I lose. Scissor cuts paper: this is strips, this is not even paper, this can take me forever to put this back together - you got me. Paper covers rock: rock is fine, no structural damage to rock. Rock can break through paper at any point, just say the word. Paper sucks.

Joke by demetri martin

MEMBERSHIP TO THE
WORLD ROCK PAPER SCISSORS ASSOCIATION

After reading this book you are now qualified to be a member in the World Rock Paper Scissors Associaition. In order to become a member simply sign up:

www.wrpsa.com/membership

BIBLIOGRAPHY

"Advanced RPS." *World Rock Paper Scissors Society*. N.p., 29 May 2015.
Web. 01 July 2017.

"MOVIE Quote DB." *Movie Quotes Database*. N.p., n.d. Web. 01 July
2017.

"The Official Rules of Rock Paper Scissors." *World Rock Paper Scissors
Society*. N.p., 29 May 2015. Web. 01 July 2017.

"Rock Paper Scissors Championship October 13th." Retro Thing. N.p., n.d.
Web. 01 July 2017.

"Rock–paper–scissors." Wikipedia. Wikimedia Foundation, 01 July 2017.
Web. 01 July 2017.

Vogel, Carol. "Rock, Paper, Payoff: Child's Play Wins Auction House an Art
Sale." The New York Times. The New York Times, 29 Apr. 2005.
Web. 01 July 2017.

"Rock, Paper, Scissors." Math Jokes 4 Mathy Folks. N.p., 08 Mar. 2011.
Web. 01 July 2017.

Made in the USA
Middletown, DE
18 December 2018